FICTION BY JORDAN MCCOLLUM

SPY ANOTHER DAY NOVELS
I, Spy
Spy for a Spy
Tomorrow We Spy

SPY ANOTHER DAY PREQUELS
Spy Noon (novella)
Mr. Nice Spy (novella)
Spy by Night (novel)

NONFICTION BY JORDAN MCCOLLUM

Character Arcs:
Founding, forming and finishing your character's journey

WRITING CRAFT SERIES

CHARACTER SYMPATHY

creating characters your readers <u>have</u> to root for

JORDAN McCOLLUM

FOREWORD by ALICIA RASLEY

DURHAM CREST BOOKS

CHARACTER SYMPATHY © 2014 Jordan McCollum

All rights reserved. No part of this publication may be reproduced, distributed, or transmitted in any form or by any means, including photocopying, recording, or other electronic or mechanical methods, without the prior written permission of the publisher, except in the case of brief quotations embodied in critical reviews and certain other noncommercial uses permitted by copyright law.

First printing, 2014

Published by Durham Crest Books
Pleasant Grove, Utah
Set in Linux Libertine

ISBN 978-1-940096-08-7

PRINTED IN THE UNITED STATES OF AMERICA

For my children,
who teach me every day,
and sometimes allow me to return the favor.

Contents

Foreword i
Introduction iii
   Defining character sympathy iii
   Why character sympathy is important iv
   Giving the reader credit v

CHAPTER 1

Ineffective Methods of Creating Character Sympathy 1

   The character 1
      The "perfect" character 1
      The sad sack 2
   Characteristics 3
      Klutziness 4
      Physical beauty 5
   Mystery 6
   Direct characterization 7
   Actions: Save the kid 8
   Backstory 9
   Conclusion 13

CHAPTER 2

Effective Methods of Creating Character Sympathy 15

Provoking emotions 17
Strengths 17
    Avoiding the perfection cliché 19
Struggles 22
    Avoiding the sad sack cliché 25
    Inner conflict 26
The noble goal: sacrifice 27
    Establishing the noble goal 30
    Personal stakes 32
    Stakes 32
Actions: Save the cat—with a cost 34
    The price of reader sympathy 35
Environment 38
    Dramatic irony 40
Effective antagonists 41
Humor 42
Timing 43

CHAPTER 3

Examples of Character Sympathy 45

Harry Potter the sad sack 47
Superheroes, super strength 49
    Superman 49
    Batman 51

Spy Another Day—sacrifice for sympathy 53
Romeo and Juliet and Dramatic irony 54
Arabian Nights and putting it all together 56
Prickly characters 59
    Ebenezer Scrooge 59
    Sherlock Holmes 61

CHAPTER 4
Sympathy for Other Characters 65
Love interest sympathy 67
Secondary character sympathy 69
Sympathy for the devil: villain and antagonist sympathy 70

CHAPTER 5
Common Challenges to Character Sympathy 73
Unlovable characters 75
Antiheroes 76

CHAPTER 6
Keeping Character Sympathy 79
Using the character arc 81
    Defeat versus failure 82
Actions to avoid 82
When the character must do something bad 83

    Clear motivations 83
    Motivations and backstory 84
    Humanizing bad actions 86

Concluding on Character Sympathy 89

References 91
    Works cited 91
    Examples cited 92
    Further reading 94

Index 96

FOREWORD

CHARACTER SYMPATHY=READER ENJOYMENT

In my childhood reading of comic books, I was surprised to find myself rooting for the bad-tempered Batman over the pure-hearted Superman. I was, after all, a parochial schoolgirl, trained to be and to revere "goodness." But Supey just didn't do it for me. That was my first lesson in the conundrum of character sympathy. There's no easy one-to-one correlation between character perfection and our perception of them.

In fact, being perfect can actually make a character unsympathetic. As Jordan points out in this book, if Superman didn't have his awkward alter-ego Clark Kent, we probably wouldn't like him much at all. She points out that the main problem with perfection is its predictability. We aren't led to like characters who always do what's required of them, but rather those who do better and/or worse than expected.

Jordan even has examples for some out-and-out villains that have gotten readers' and viewers' sympathy over the years. I've got a few others that show the human capacity to empathize with the imperfect. If we didn't have that embracing empathy, we'd never have identified with a ruthless usurper (Macbeth), a whiny kid (Holden Caulfield), an ungrateful runaway and a conman (Wizard of Oz), a manipulative super-narcissist (Gone Girl), two

Character Sympathy

escaping killers (Thelma and Louise), a suicidal loser (It's a Wonderful Life), and the original devil himself (Paradise Lost). Just as we so often fall in love with the "wrong" person, we often identify with the "wrong" character—and writers have to figure out why and how.

Character sympathy puts the reader into the character's mind and heart. But in the broader sense, it happens because the writer can identify with the reader, figuring out what will appeal and what will appall—and know why those two are not always rational or laudable.

"Why and how" are what Jordan is exploring here, with her excellent mix of psychological insights and her practical suggestions for creating (and modifying) characters to increase reader identification. I'd suggest reading this book before you start writing a novel, and then again as you're revising the first draft. Then you can have Jordan's principles in mind as you create the characters, and can use later the practical tips to improve the identifiability of their motivations and actions.

Best of luck, and most of all, have fun with your characters! That's what we want our for our readers, after all!

Alicia Rasley

RITA-award-winning and best-selling novelist of *The Year She Fell*

Fiction-writing teacher and author of *The Story Within* plot guide

Introduction

Defining Character Sympathy

At first glance, it might seem character sympathy is simply getting our readers to like our character or feel pity for him. However, character sympathy runs deeper than simply liking a character. Although the term "sympathy" might be misconstrued to mean "pity," character sympathy also goes beyond a reader feeling sorry for our characters.

Instead, we're hoping to make our readers feel what our character feels and root for our character to achieve her goals. Merriam-Webster's online dictionary summarizes the definition of sympathy with these important points:
- the feeling that you care about and are sorry about someone else's trouble, grief, misfortune, etc.
- a feeling of support for something
- a state in which different people share the same interests, opinions, goals, etc.

We want our readers to support our character and her quest and goals. We want our readers to share those goals. And most of all, we want our readers to care about our character's troubles, problems and journey to accomplishing these goals—because if they don't care, they won't have any desire to read about that journey!

Sympathy in this sense is truly feeling what the character

feels, worrying over the same things he worries about, and wanting him to succeed against all odds. If we can get our readers to fully sympathize and identify with our character, our readers will enjoy that journey with our character and then clamor for more.

Why Character Sympathy is Important

A "sympathetic" character is one the reader can relate to. The reader feels the things he feels, and the reader understands the difficulties that character is going through.

Often when we think of character sympathy as love or envy or pity, but at its core, what our fiction really needs is at least one character the reader can root for and relate to. When we have a character our readers can really care about, even if they don't love the character, your readers will be fully engaged in your story and beg for more.

It may seem like sympathizing with a main character (who isn't a villain or an antihero, at least) is automatic—but anyone who's ever written an unsympathetic character quickly learns that it's not. Sometimes we writers think we're doing something avant-garde by creating someone as alienated, sarcastic, apathetic or distant as a "real" person—but most of the time, we learn that this "cutting-edge" technique has been tried before. Without success.

On the other hand, sometimes we just neglect to actively create that character sympathy—and it *is* something we

INTRODUCTION

have to actively create most of the time. The technique is not difficult to master, but without our readers' identification, our character will be flat, unlikeable and uninteresting. When we employ the techniques of character sympathy, we foster a sympathetic feeling within our readers to truly draw them into the story.

I'm using "sympathetic character" as shorthand for "a character whom the reader can identify with." Creating reader identification—character sympathy—is the ultimate goal here, because, as James N. Frey says in *How to Write a Damn Good Novel, II*, a character the reader can identify with is the key to creating the fictive dream, to immersing the reader into the world of the story (not to mention the mind of the character). He concludes, "Sympathy is the doorway through which the reader gains emotional access to a story. Without sympathy, the reader has no emotional involvement in the story" (9-10).

I delved into researching the techniques to create character sympathy effectively because I've done it all wrong before. The underlying principles are simple, but it's still easy to miss the mark unless we make a conscious effort to create that sympathy.

GIVING THE READER CREDIT

I think it's important to give the reader some credit before we begin. Sometimes we're inclined to think readers will only root for, or identify and sympathize with, characters who are good, or heroic, or at least similar to the readers themselves. Granted, most readers probably *would* sympathize with a character who's a carbon copy of them. However, it's pretty hard to write a new book for each and every reader.

Most readers are sophisticated enough to sympathize with a character who is nothing like them. With careful engineering on the part of the author, most readers can also sympathize with a character who does everything objectionable and who is *not* good. A reader doesn't have to like a character to understand him, identify with him or sympathize with him.

At its heart, character sympathy comes from focusing on the things that make our character similar to our readers: her strengths and weaknesses, his struggles and inner conflict, and most of all, her action that carries her toward growth and his sacrifices for another person. Attempts to force the reader to like our character by making her super- or subhuman will almost always backfire. Instead, we must dig into some of the universal attributes of the experience of simply being *human* to help our readers relate to our character.

Laying out the map

In this book, we'll start by looking at methods of creating character sympathy that don't work before we dig into methods that do. Because identification is built using several intertwining techniques, a few character examples are collected in their own chapter, showing how they build sympathy with the reader in the course of their stories. Next, we'll look at building sympathy for

INTRODUCTION

secondary and other characters. Then we'll focus on some common challenges for reader identification, such as unlovable characters and antiheroes. We'll wrap up with a discussion on keeping character sympathy once we've established it.

Ineffective Methods of Creating Character Sympathy

Some "classic" attempts at character sympathy are merely clichés.

Creating reader identification with our characters is no accident, and if we leave it up to chance, there's a good chance we may fall into tired tropes that have been used so often that they're no longer effective. If we want our readers to really root for our characters, we should make sure to avoid these ineffective methods of creating character sympathy.

THE CHARACTER

Character sympathy naturally must start with the character herself. Many times, however, we fall into clichéd character traps or ineffective patterns to "force" our readers to love our character. We work so hard to make the character irresistible that we accidentally make the character unrealistic—and unlovable.

The "perfect" character

Often one of the earliest attempts we make at character sympathy is creating a character who's perfect. Who wouldn't love someone who can juggle three children's homeschooling, piano, dance and yoga schedules; a full-time, fulfilling job; an extremely attractive and adventurous husband; caring for the homeless at the soup kitchen; teaching ESL adults to read; rescuing shelter puppies; and running her Etsy shop and craft blog?

Who wouldn't love her? Probably everyone who can't do all that. Like 99.9% of the population.

If our major objective in creating character sympathy is to

get readers to identify with our character and her goal, creating a character so much better than our readers is not a good start. Characters who are too perfect are impossible for readers to identify with.

A perfect character also has no room for a character arc. Having already attained perfection three times this week, the character has no need to grow and change throughout the course of the story. While some stories do not feature character arcs, the protagonists of those stories are typically either already familiarly flawed (non-arcing characters) or about to face major temptation ("flat" character arc). And even these characters must gain readers' sympathy in other ways.

The perfect character needs some flaws to gain readers' sympathy. But it's easy to swing to the other extreme in trying to create that sympathy.

The sad sack
Sometimes, instead of going for the perfect character, we try to use a character the reader can't help but sympathize with because of his horrible situation, or his awful life. We keep the villains coming at him and keep tearing him down until he can be brought no lower—and then we pull out the rug. Who wouldn't sympathize with someone so put upon? It may seem like readers will *have* to love him.

While it's always fun for us to put the screws to our characters, the danger here is piling on the pain so deep that our characters are left as victims, immobilized by all

Ineffective Methods of Creating Character Sympathy

their problems, especially early on in the book. "A passive victim doesn't struggle—just suffers," as editor and RITA-award winning author Alicia Rasley puts it in her article "Sympathy without Saintliness." "Defeat isn't sympathetic. It's pathetic."

The character can even begin to actively turn off your readers if he notes his own horrible, unending fate, while still doing nothing to fight it. The first few times we see the cartoon character Eeyore, we pity him. But eventually, we recognize the pattern: when something bad befalls him, it's just another thing piled on—and that's exactly how he sees these negative events. He can't escape his horrible fate and accepts it, with passive-aggressive complaints. When our characters' complaining turns to playing the victim or whining, we're driving away readers. It may be good for occasional comic relief, but not many readers would want to spend three hundred pages seeing the world through Eeyore's eyes.

When it comes to sympathetic characters, sad sacks need not apply.

CHARACTERISTICS

Once we've avoided the perfect and pathetic extremes, we must steer clear of other common shortcuts to character sympathy. While these techniques may still be marginally effective, the paths to these "shortcuts" are so well-worn that they're quickly becoming clichés as well.

Klutziness

Often a character, especially a woman, is portrayed as a klutz, stumbling into the hero's arms and attempting to do the same to readers' hearts. Or perhaps she says things she shouldn't, sharing her own embarrassing internal monologue about the attractiveness of the man she's talking to with him. This trope is used more every day.

It *is* natural for readers to sympathize with someone who's embarrassed. They've been there and they understand what it feels like. It's an easy gimmick to succumb to, which is why klutzy heroines are so popular right now.

However, klutziness can also be a "cheat" for writers. It's a characteristic that's often tacked on without a deeper relationship to the character's personality and movement. While it can be funny to see a ballerina who bumps into things offstage, if she's klutzy only when the plot demands, the clumsiness is pure shtick. It can quickly become tiresome.

A friend once received feedback that her character's lack of coordination felt like the author was trying too hard to make the reader love the character. Any characteristic might be taken to this extreme and create a negative reaction to the manipulation.

Keep your character's reader identification tied to something inherent in the character and her actions instead of a gimmick.

INEFFECTIVE METHODS OF CREATING CHARACTER SYMPATHY

Physical beauty

Playing on a character's attractiveness to create character sympathy is the descriptive equivalent of relying on perfection to make your character sympathetic. Often characters are beautiful and yet perfectly modest about it, and readers have to rely on other characters informing us of the character's beauty. And they do. A lot. The more the heroine protests, outlining her flaws (her nose is too straight and she has! A! *Freckle*!), the more people around her insist she's gorgeous and wonder how she can possibly not see it.

This doesn't just apply to women, either. We've all seen dozens of broad-shouldered heroes or perfectly precocious cherub children. When the character's description feels like a blatant ploy to make the reader fall for a character, it probably is.

While occasionally in real life, we may instantly like a child (or an attractive adult) based on his or her appearance, if that person does nothing to deserve our affection, the feeling doesn't last. The same is true of reader identification—physical beauty simply doesn't run deep enough to create lasting character sympathy by itself.

This doesn't mean all your characters have to be disfigured—just that physical beauty shouldn't play into your plan to build character sympathy.

Mystery

Sometimes we attempt to conceal the things that will create the most sympathy with our character in order to generate suspense about her.

Suspense is an important tool and it does propel readers through a story. However, it's not effective if the readers don't care about the characters, and keeping the reader in suspense about *why* they should care about the character will usually backfire. If we conceal the aspects of our character that are necessary to develop our reader's identification with her, we risk losing those readers long before they discover those reasons.

It's difficult for readers to sit through chapter after chapter of inexplicable, inexcusable actions from the main character. If we neglect developing character sympathy first, it's too easy to make a reader feel like he or she is being dragged through the plot points by an emotionless alien.

For example, if the Disney movie *Frozen* began when Elsa and Anna were estranged adults without explaining why Elsa suddenly drew away from her sister, it would have created more of a sense of mystery about Elsa and a bigger surprise when her ice powers are revealed. However, viewers would've had less sympathy for Elsa, no matter how much backstory we tried to add in later, and the filmmakers knew viewers needed to sympathize with Elsa for the story to work.

INEFFECTIVE METHODS OF CREATING CHARACTER SYMPATHY

That isn't to say we have to explain absolutely everything our character does immediately. But most readers won't sit through a hundred pages of the protagonist's self-destructive, cruel, or evil behavior to get to the reasons they're supposed to care about the character. We must use other methods to generate sympathy first before we develop the suspense about the character's true motivations and feelings.

DIRECT CHARACTERIZATION

Sometimes we attempt to build character sympathy by showing how good he is another way: by having the other characters tell us this. This method of direct characterization has two almost insurmountable challenges: it's resorting to telling instead of showing, and it's another version of the too-perfect character.

We've already established that perfect characters aren't sympathetic. They are so much better than the reader that it's difficult to relate to them, and without flaws, they lack a compelling character journey. Having other characters praise the main character is a variation on this theme. While readers might give some small amount of credence to these characters' judgment, they are acutely aware that these other characters are all part of the author's design and can see through this. But worse, instead of showing us the character's perfection, we have other characters *tell* about it.

Most of all, instead of *telling* the reader the character is deserving of sympathy, we must *show* the reader. Others'

Character Sympathy

descriptions of the main character are never as convincing or compelling to readers as watching what the main character *does*. So while his friends may praise his generosity and kindness, if readers only see the hero kicking puppies, they won't believe the other characters. In fiction, as in life, actions speak louder than words.

Sometimes a third party showing this kind of love for the character helps boost sympathy, but the effect is so small that it cannot be the sole method for creating character sympathy. After all, even serial killers can find love or have a parent or sibling who loved them. Our characters must try harder to earn the reader's identification.

ACTIONS: SAVE THE KID

A character's actions should be paramount in creating character sympathy. However, that doesn't mean we can choose just any actions to create reader identification.

Often, the first ideas that spring to mind are actions no reader could resist: saving a child or a house pet, or some other heroic act. Heroism on that scale in the real world receives so much attention because the circumstances that create that kind of action are rare. But this method backfires in creating character sympathy.

Alicia Rasley lists "Putting in an unrelated incident where [the protagonist] is kind to someone or saves someone's life" under ineffective ways to create character sympathy in her article "Sympathy without Saintliness." She continues, "While of course, if the heroine saves

Ineffective Methods of Creating Character Sympathy

someone's life in the first scene, we're going to probably think well of her, but only if we don't feel it's manipulative. And if there's no real connection to the plot, if this life-saving event doesn't lead to some plot development, we'll know that was just stuck in to manipulate us."

In fiction, unlike in real life, readers are acutely aware that someone is manipulating the story events. The protagonist's heroic acts may even feel less like we writers are manipulating the plot, and more like we're manipulating the reader, undermining identification.

Worse, we might make the heroic act itself too easy—not that the act is inherently easy, but that the character does it quickly and without any internal conflict or external struggle.

Even less effective, these heroic acts may have taken place before the story begins. Backstory is another tactic for creating character sympathy that's become a cliché.

Backstory

Whenever someone asks "How can I make this character (especially a villain) more sympathetic?", it seems like the first answer to pop up is "Give him a tragic backstory!" While it's true that a difficult childhood can make readers pity the character, it's difficult to build true reader sympathy using backstory.

One of the main uses for backstory is to justify the

character's unsympathetic behavior, attitudes and actions. We show them growing up, or use flashbacks and memories to show the injustices they've suffered. His father was always at work, his mother denied him jelly on his peanut butter sandwiches, his first girlfriend dumped him for a jerk, his first wife cheated on him, his boss doesn't recognize his work, even his dog doesn't appreciate him.

Not only is this overdone, but, frankly, it's lazy storytelling. Rather than work on character sympathy in the character's present story, we hope that some heroic act or tragedy in his past will force the reader to identify with them.

The tragic backstory as a method of creating character sympathy these days is more likely to induce eye-rolls and groans than tug at our readers' heartstrings. As readers trudge through the laundry list of reasons they "should" feel sorry for the character, not only are we making a vast logical leap—that pitying the character is the same thing as identifying with them—but eventually these efforts just begin to feel unrealistic, and the character becomes merely a vehicle for all these piled-on tragedies.

This tired trope is so clichéd that even children's shows mock it. In the animated television show *Phineas and Ferb*, geared at kids five to eight years old, the villain virtually always explains his evil "-inator" device with a tragic backstory. These backstories include everything from a hardscrabble childhood to perpetually losing at the science fair, from his parents' obsessive favoritism of his

INEFFECTIVE METHODS OF CREATING CHARACTER SYMPATHY

younger brother to eventually being abandoned and adopted by ocelots. The "-inators" inventions relate thematically to the backstory in outlandish ways, and the entire premise is a running gag played for humor—for young children.

A character like the villain of *Phineas and Ferb* is trapped in his past, refusing to move forward. Unless this is a specific part of the character's arc, a character caught under this mountain of backstory can be painful to watch. The character insists on dredging up their own painful past to flagellate themselves again and again. Rather than creating identification between our readers and our characters, we can quickly hit the "emotional safety valve," where our readers' emotional overload results in turning off their own strong emotions as a measure of self-preservation.

Rasley summarizes the principle at work here in "Sympathy and Saintliness": "While we want to sympathize with the characters, we don't want them to be victims so battered by past events that they don't actually live in the present."

A failure to live and act in the present sets up difficult obstacles to overcome in establishing character sympathy. If our stories or our characters remain trapped in the past, we are robbing our readers of the opportunity to get to know the character in the present. We must focus on the events of the story, because only our character's actions in the present truly influence character sympathy.

Character Sympathy

Mystery Man on Film discussed this principle when he blogged about the *Raiders of the Lost Ark* story conference between George Lucas, Steven Spielberg and Laurence Kasdan (creator, director and screenwriter, respectively). Mystery Man noted that the trio discussed Indiana Jones's relationship with Marion Ravenswood. They liked the idea that she was underage during their first romantic encounter, in the backstory, but they balked at the idea of Indy plotting to steal the pendant from her in the present story, worried that it would undercut Indy's sympathy with the audience.

Mystery Man concludes, "What happens in the past, off screen, good or bad, does not affect sympathy. It's what we see the character do in the present that determines how much we will or will not care about that character." Backstory—whether the character was a war hero or came through childhood with battle scars—is no match for watching the character's actions in the present, where true sympathy is won and lost.

This is not to say that our characters have to have had perfect lives, or that we should never have any backstory. Backstory can definitely influence how our characters are and act—they had to come from somewhere! We all have our past heartaches and problems, and those heartaches may influence the story—but most likely they'll influence it by setting up a character arc, creating character attitudes and motivating character action in the present. Backstory isn't enough to make a reader care.

CONCLUSION

These methods are ineffective at creating reader sympathy for a number of reasons. Many of them are so overused that they have become clichés, which are so familiar the reader glosses over them instead of fully engage with the character. Several of these methods portray the character as something more than or less than human, either a perfect person, or a pathetic excuse for one. We've established that neither of these are sympathetic.

However, the most essential reason why these methods fail is that we're trying to *force* the reader to think and feel a certain way. While evoking a specific emotional response may be the ultimate goal of fiction, if we go into our stories with reader manipulation as the agenda, our readers can often tell. Our readers are too savvy to fall for the tired tropes that might have been effective for creating character sympathy once upon a time.

Instead of forcing our readers to love our characters, as writers we should focus on the character himself, and what he *does* to deserve our readers' identification. Because it's not just the aspects of his psyche, but what our character *does* that truly defines him for the reader. When we can show the reader that the character is worthy of their identification—instead of telling or ordering them to identify with the character (because he's kind to kittens!)—our character becomes truly worthy of real sympathy.

Effective Methods of Creating Character Sympathy

Now that we've covered what doesn't work
to create character sympathy,
let's dig into what we need to do
to generate reader identification.

Provoking emotions

In his first writing craft book, *How to Write a Damn Good Novel*, James N. Frey argues that the first step in creating reader identification is to "give your reader an emotional touchstone" (110). To do this, you must "plunge a character into an emotion-provoking situation" (110). The emotion doesn't have to be positive—Frey lists pity, contempt and fear as examples.

Provoking emotions is the ultimate goal of creating reader identification: we want them to care about the character and her outcome. While there are many, many techniques for promoting character sympathy, no single technique is usually sufficient to produce the full effect on its own. The most powerful way to engage the reader's emotions and create character sympathy is by using a combination of strengths, struggles and sacrifice.

Strengths

All characters must have some strength. I'm sure you know that doesn't mean they have to be able to bench-press a Beemer. Instead, there has to be some strength of character, some inner resource, some poise—something to show the readers why they would want to sympathize with, or look up to, or just flat out *be* this person.

Although physical strength might count, a character's strength is usually more than just muscles. Skills, such as being good at their chosen hobby or profession, fall under strengths, as well. But more than that, a character's strength is something indomitable within her.

Character Sympathy

Outer strengths are typically easy to find by looking at whatever the character is uniquely good at. Inner strengths can be more tricky. To find your character's inner strength, ask yourself what makes him get up in the morning? What is her ultimate goal in life? What does he do when his wife is in danger and all hope of saving her is lost? How does she react when someone comes between her and the man she loves? What does he do (or want to do) when his boss/his mother/the woman he loves says, "Take a hike"?

The answer isn't going to be the same for every character—but few readers really want to spend eight or more hours in the head of someone who would answer "nothing" to any one of those questions. While readers do understand someone who struggles, someone with a sad past, someone facing a difficult choice, letting your character just roll over and take it is intensely frustrating to a reader.

Many characteristics count as a character strength, including:
- Perseverance
- Self-control
- Skill
- Optimism
- Self-sacrifice
- Wit or humor
- Integrity

However, any one of these, or any combination of them,

can verge into the "too-perfect" realm if they're not tempered with struggles.

Avoiding the perfection cliché

A character who's easily and confidently stronger than every challenge he faces isn't really sympathetic. He's static with nowhere to grow. We read to see that character growth—and that character growth is where we become most sympathetic with those characters.

When a character is all strength, he takes everything in stride, and everything continually works out for him. Here's an example of how this works:

> Jeremy stared at the flames leaping from the third-story windows. There were three children unaccounted for. He took a deep breath and barreled through the open doorway, up the stairs, around corner after corner. The distant cries for help finally reached his ears over the cacophonous crackling. The children—they were trapped behind a locked door.
>
> He threw his full weight against the door. It splintered at the massive force. He scooped up the children, two in his right, one his is left, and ran back down the stairs.
>
> Jeremy gasped for a cool breath as he burst through the doorway to the outside. The headmistress held out her arms for a child and he held out one of them, smudged and bedraggled but alive. She clutched the boy to her chest, her eyes shining with admiration. "You're our hero," she said.

Character Sympathy

Jeremy's strong, brave, and courageous. He'll get a key to the city for his heroism. But he isn't very interesting or sympathetic. I think most people would like to think they'd be willing to help someone in danger. Everything works out really easily for Jeremy. He's strong enough, he's brave enough, and doggone it, people like him. He never really doubts his ability to perform an extraordinary feat.

Without struggles, opposition and internal conflict, the reader has little to sympathize with. Let's try another rescue story with more struggles to see how that affects how we see our main character, Timothy:

> Timothy walked into his boss's office. Jim waited behind his desk and gestured for Timothy to take the seat across from him. Timothy's stomach sank. Jim knew. He had to know. Timothy had screwed up on the last quarter's figures, and it was going to cost the company big—but first, it'd cost Timothy even bigger.
> "I wanted to talk to you," Jim said. "After all the time you put in on last quarter's numbers, I think you really deserve this."
> Here it came. Jim slid an envelope across the desk. Timothy's pulse slowed in his ears, but he managed to open it.
> Wait, what? Instead of a pink slip . . . a check. Timothy looked up to Jim.
> "You've saved the company millions by catching that typo in the Smith account. You deserve it."

But Denise was the one who'd caught that mistake, not him. "What about Denise? She worked a lot of overtime, too."

Jim snorted. "She screwed up the final numbers. Whenever she decides to come back into the office, she'll get what she deserved, too."

Timothy's palms turned clammy. Denise was home with a sick kid—and that error was his fault. Could he let her take the fall?

No, he had to tell the truth. Didn't he?

Timothy clutched his envelope tighter. He could think about this and figure out a way to make it right without sacrificing anything. Denise wouldn't be in until—

The secretary knocked at the door before poking her head in. "Mr. Carson, Denise just got here."

"Send her in." Jim picked up the other envelope on his desk and tapped it on his fingertips. "You can go, Timothy."

Timothy stood. He could walk out of here. It would be so easy. He could keep his job and his check. He was safe.

But he couldn't throw Denise under the bus. She was the only person in the office who'd ever been nice to him. "Um, Mr. Carson?"

Jim looked up, one eyebrow quirked. "Don't worry, Timothy. None of this will reflect on you, I'll make sure of it."

This was his chance. He could leave now, scot-free, no consequences. It would be wrong, but it would save his job, feed his family for another two

CHARACTER SYMPATHY

> weeks. He'd be the only one who knew the truth. He turned for the door—
> No. He turned back. "It wasn't Denise's mistake, Mr. Carson. It was mine."

Timothy's challenges aren't as physically daunting as Jeremy's were. Timothy doesn't have to break down a door or carry out three orphans to impress us—he just has to overcome difficulties and insecurities, his internal struggle, to do the right thing even when it hurts him.

STRUGGLES

While sympathetic characters must have strength, they need more than just moral or physical perfection to get readers onboard. For readers to truly identify with him, a character needs to struggle. (I doubt I need to clarify this, but just in case: struggling with how incredibly awesome he is doesn't count.)

In *How to Write a Damn Good Novel, II,* James N. Frey goes so far as to say that you have to make the reader feel sorry for the character. I don't know that I'd say that—but I would say that you have to let the reader see your character struggling. That's essentially what Frey conveys—let the reader see the character as lonely, disadvantaged, put upon, sad, confused, unpopular, unfulfilled, imperiled, etc. The reader doesn't have to pity the character to identify with him.

We've established that being mired in the terrible past

Effective Methods of Creating Character Sympathy

isn't a good way to create character sympathy, so we need another kind of struggle, one more directly tied to the plot. For example, the character might work against an antagonist, whether a person or an impersonal force. The antagonist, especially at the beginning, should actually win. We're cultured to side with the underdog, the Cinderella story, the person who has been wronged. Failure can contribute to sympathy as well as move the plot forward.

The antagonist may be a supervillain, but more likely, the antagonist is simply someone who stands in the way of our hero's goals. Thus this struggle may be an epic battle or a smaller, more personal loss. In her article "Sympathy without Saintliness," Alicia Rasley uses the example of the famous heroine Scarlett O'Hara:

> Whether we like Scarlett O'Hara or not (and we probably don't early in the book), we sympathize with her when her impassioned declaration to Ashley (and his wussy rejection of her) turns out to be overheard by, of all people, the arrogant Rhett Butler. The anguish . . . the embarrassment! We know just how she feels, and somehow we feel even more because our sympathy is unwilling, because we don't WANT to identify with this snotty little flirt. And we don't identify with her . . . that is, until something bad happens to her that we can actually imagine happening to us.
>
> The key is—we have to know what it's like, or be able to imagine what it's like, to be in this situation.

Character Sympathy

> But there's more. The character has to squirm. The character has to be in difficulty. The character has to care.

Having the readers imagine living through this difficult situation helps them to identify with the character—but even more, the reader needs to see that the character himself cares about his life and his results rather than rolling over to accept another horrible fate.

Several types of struggles "count" for creating character sympathy, including:
- Resisting the call to adventure
- Self-doubt
- Embarrassment
- Being weaker than the antagonist
- Loneliness
- Fear

No matter what kind of struggles our character faces, make sure that the character is invested enough in her goal that she must push forward, even though each setback does affect her personally. The character must care if we want the reader to care, too.

Just as strengths alone aren't interesting, struggles by themselves aren't sufficient to create character sympathy. Struggle without strength turns our character into a sad sack, and makes him not compelling to read about.

However, the most sympathetic character isn't struggling

solely against (obviously evil) external antagonists—the hero must also have internal conflict. Some of the greatest, most compelling characters are those that struggle against some part of them that doesn't want to do what he knows he should—for reasons the reader knows and understands (it's hard, it risks life and limb, etc.).

Avoiding the sad sack cliché

One of the first techniques we master in creating sympathetic characters is knowing that characters have to have problems. And they have to be major problems—something that they'll really struggle with, things that appear insurmountable. The temptation, then, can be to take that to the extreme. If some suffering makes our character sympathetic, we reason, doesn't a lot of suffering make her even more sympathetic?

Not always. Sometimes, as they say, more is just more.

Too many difficulties, past or present, make it harder and harder for the reader to sympathize with our character. She begin to feel less like a real person and more like a laundry list of problems. To borrow an analogy from socioeconomics, if you had one bee sting, you would most certainly take care of it. But if you had six or ten or twenty bee stings, fixing just one of them isn't going to make a big difference in your overall pain level. Likewise, if your character's got ninety-nine problems, readers care less and less about resolving one.

So it's not really difficulties themselves, past or present, that make a character sympathetic. What really generates character sympathy is observing how the characters react. They're not indifferent to their problems—they definitely need to feel the pain. But they're also not self-pitying or whining about them, or, worst of all, passively dwelling on and submitting to them and even more injustice for no apparent reason. As Frey puts it:

> Whenever a reader experiences profound empathy with a character, it is because the character is in the throes of intense inner conflict. A character may be in the most pathetic straits in the history of literature, but if he has no inner conflict, the only emotional response the writer can expect from the reader is pity. (*How to Write a Damn Good Novel, II*, 36-37)

And pity is not our goal! Our character must show that inner strength that the readers admired from the first. She has to be able to lift her head after the wickedest defeat and say "I'll never go hungry again!" (Or something original and pertinent to your story.)

Inner conflict

To earn readers' sympathy, our character must do more than struggle against external forces—they should battle internally, too. Once we have the readers feeling what the character is feeling, then we can use internal conflict to fully transport the reader into the character's head and the world of the story.

James N. Frey points out in *How to Write a Damn Good Novel* that "true identification can occur only when the characters face choices *so that the reader can participate in the decision-making process*. . . . Identification comes when the reader pulls for the character to make the right choices" (111, emphasis in original).

As writers, we have the opportunity to design our character's choices to help create this inner conflict. Rather than making it easy for our hero to do the right thing, we can work on making it more difficult for him to make the right choice. Readers don't have as much of a chance to sympathize with the lawyer who immediately takes the charity case versus the one who really can't afford to take the charity case, which is a long shot even on the best day—but the case is so deserving and they need help so badly that our hero can't resist, even if it means another month of Ramen noodles.

Struggles in only external problems don't engage the reader as fully as watching our character in a moral dilemma. If we give him tough choices, conflicting motivations, and soul-wrenching challenges, we give him the opportunity to connect with the reader on an emotional level.

THE NOBLE GOAL: SACRIFICE

Once we've established the character's strengths and balanced them with struggles, the next step to ensuring reader identification is to get the reader to support the character's goals and aspirations. The character himself

Character Sympathy

doesn't necessarily have to be someone the reader would admire, but the character's goals should be something the reader can believe in.

Readers need a reason to root for the character and hope for his success. Even a despicable degenerate can win readers over if we can sympathize with his goal—or his motivations. In *How to Write a Damn Good Novel, II*, James N. Frey says the easiest way to get readers to support a character's goal is to make sure the goal is noble. To qualify as a noble goal or motivation, often we use something that helps society, something that's self-sacrificing, something that benefits another person more than it does the main character.

Frey's example is of a convict who wants to escape prison. Most readers would probably say they want people who've committed crimes to stay behind bars. You could experiment with having the convict be wrongfully accused, but Frey argues that the surer way to create reader identification is to make the motivations behind the goals—which may seem selfish on the surface—look more selfless. His convict's goal is to escape prison not just because he wants freedom right now, but because he wants to make amends and become a better person. Better still, we could make his goal to help someone else.

I've seen this technique work even in real life. The opening of one of my favorite game shows always featured short biographies of the four competitors, wherein they almost always predicted their ultimate victory and gloated about how much better they were than the competition (whom they'd never met).

In one episode, I was all set to really dislike one competitor after the usual boasting in her introduction, and then they asked her what she'd do with the prize money. She planned to put a down payment on a home in Brooklyn. It's not a great humanitarian vision. It's not even anything all that remarkable. It's just the run-of-the-mill American dream. But she didn't just want a home for the sake of fulfilling the picket-fences plan that's been programmed into us—she wanted to be able to buy a home in a good area of Brooklyn so her daughter could go to the best school in the city.

That was all it took for me to root for her. The prize money could have gone a long way to establishing her own restaurant, or toward travel, bills or savings. But when this woman, this mother, put her child's betterment above her own, I was on her side in a flash. I was all ready to root against her until she had a noble goal.

Note that this goal isn't about the betterment of society. It's still kind of self-centered, providing for her own child and excelling at her parental responsibilities. But because it's focused on another person's needs—especially a child's—it still helps that character appear sympathetic.

Sometimes focusing on another person is even better than a general desire to help humanity to foster character sympathy. Improving society can be too vague: helping one specific person, such as the character's child, can actually be more effective as a character goal than trying to better the whole world.

At its core, the noble goal isn't about doing something for the greater good, making the planet a better place or achieving world peace. The noble goal shows that our character is capable of caring about someone or something else more than he cares about himself. It shows readers that the character has the capacity to see others' needs and problems, and that, for at least this one instance, he can set aside the selfish impulses we all have and think of someone else. Even if it's the only glimpse readers have of the character's potential for growth, it's an important one.

Establishing the noble goal

The character's immediate goal at the outset of the story may not meet the classic definition of "noble." Establishing the character's noble goal early on is important, but we don't have to show the character's ultimate goal of the story on page one. However, the more objectionable the character's early actions might be to the reader, the more important it is to establish a noble motivation behind those actions as early as we can.

Early in my writing career, I wrote a book with an unsympathetic main character. In the opening chapter, she was secretly the forger-artist behind a fake show of posthumously discovered works by a famous artist. Not fully revealed initially, her major motivation behind this deceit was to build her own art career in the future. While my beta readers found the mystery of her participation in

Effective Methods of Creating Character Sympathy

the show intriguing, that alone was not enough to create sympathy with the character.

It wasn't the character's objectionable actions that undermined my readers' identification with her. If she'd done the exact same actions with a less selfish purpose, my readers would probably not have been put off. I tried a number of other factors to increase her sympathy—adding more self-doubts, struggles and inner conflict—but the lack of a noble goal continued to undermine identification. I could've addressed this directly if, instead, she was participating in the show to bring the real artist the recognition he deserved. Better still, I could've somehow tied her success in the show to benefit someone else more directly, someone she cares about, someone whose fate will be affected far more than a dead artist.

When the character begins with end-goal for the story at the outset, it can be easier to tie the character's immediate actions to that noble end-goal. However, often the character doesn't start off his story working toward that goal. Instead, he learns over time and takes on a larger quest or journey of growth. We need a smaller-scale goal with noble motivations to satisfy reader sympathy at the outset, or rely on other methods to build reader identification.

The character may resist this goal change, the call to adventure or action. Most likely, they're avoiding a noble goal. Naturally, their reasons for doing so are usually self-centered—they're afraid—but we can also use noble goals to increase the inner conflict of accepting the call to action. Our character may be afraid of leaving the Shire, but perhaps he's also afraid of leaving his invalid friend without a caretaker. These personal stakes can help to develop even deeper character sympathy.

Personal stakes

Another reason why a noble goal is so important for establishing reader sympathy is that it creates personal stakes for our character that will influence their actions throughout the story. The character needs a reason to go on the journey of the story—a journey of growth and change that's sure to be difficult. Growth for its own sake isn't compelling in fiction. By creating these personal stakes, we help our readers become invested in the character's journey.

The term personal stakes doesn't mean the character's journey only affects him. Personal stakes are more than just internal stakes. Certainly, if our character chooses not to grow, he'll probably suffer. But if he's the only one suffering, no one around him—including the reader—has much of a reason to care. If we can attach greater consequences to the character's success, affecting someone outside of him, we give the reader an even greater investment in the outcome as we increase the stakes.

Stakes

Our stories may have both "public stakes," to borrow Donald Maass's terminology, and "personal stakes."

In *The Breakout Novelist*, Maass defines public stakes as

"what society as a whole might lose should the outcome of the story prove unfavorable" (18). Many genres demand high public stakes, but other stories become melodramatic with high public stakes. The fate of the world usually doesn't hang in the balance in a family saga—and if it did, readers might have to choose between caring about whether the daughter ever finds her place in the family or saves the world.

Public stakes may be important to the constraints of our genre, but personal stakes are vital to all characters. There must be something the character is at risk of losing, or losing out on. This gives not only the character but the reader something to *care* about. As Maass says, "Readers care because the protagonist cares. In other words, to the degree that your main character feels passionately invested in his own life, readers will feel invested, too" (22). As we show what the character cares about and is invested in, we can use these things to increase his inner conflict and sacrifices.

The stakes in the opening scenes, personal and public, will usually not be the same as at the climax. Continuing to escalate these stakes throughout the book helps to keep readers' interest and sympathy. As we engineer these increasing stakes, we can raise the threat, and force the character to sacrifice more.

When the character makes a sacrifice for someone or something he values more than himself, he creates and keeps reader identification.

ACTIONS: SAVE THE CAT—WITH A COST

Once we've done all we can to establish our character's strengths and struggles, we must be sure to let them act. Ultimately, reader identification is best won and lost through the character's actions (which is also how we show struggles and strength). As we've already learned from Mystery Man on Film, "It's what we see the character do in the present that determines how much we will or will not care about that character."

Screenwriters focus on this idea especially, because character action is all they have to work with. Screenwriter Blake Snyder believed this element of action to create character sympathy was so important, he named his book of screenwriting principles after it: *Save the Cat!* However, the title is a little misleading. Taken out of context, it sounds like we're being urged to throw in some unrelated heroic act early in the course of the work to make the reader like the character.

That isn't what Snyder advocates. He defines the principle as "The hero has to *do* something when we meet him so that we like him and want him to win" (121).

Note that the actual rule doesn't state the act has to be particularly heroic, or unrelated to the plot, or actually involve felines. It's simply a principle of action, to remind us that a character doesn't win our readers' hearts simply by being cool or capable or flashy, and it's as true in the latest Hollywood blockbuster as in the quietest literary novel.

EFFECTIVE METHODS OF CREATING CHARACTER SYMPATHY

Kindness to small children and animals isn't enough—just about anybody but the absolute worst psycho- or sociopath is nice to his mother and babies. Saving orphans from a burning building isn't going to be enough on its own, either.

The actions that help to create character sympathy aren't necessarily acts of heroism such as helping orphans or indigents or house pets. Character actions that induce sympathy relate directly back to the "noble" goal: they show that the character has the ability to put someone else's needs ahead of his own in some way. But more than simply stating the character's noble intentions, the character shows us in their actions that he really is capable of caring about someone else.

The price of reader sympathy

Adding an extraneous "noble" act isn't always enough to win readers' hearts, and it may not mesh well with your plot. Sometimes the best way to create character sympathy is to go a few steps further and increase the price or sacrifice of a choice they're already making within the confines of the plot. We can make it more difficult for the character to act nobly by making the right choice harder, requiring sacrifice. There are a few ways to do this, but the surest ways tap into the character's motivations.

For one method, we could have the character do the right thing—for the wrong reasons. Let's say our hero is a lawyer. He's approached with a charity case that he'd never normally take, but the defendant's mother is hot. We still have the right actions to help generate sympathy (taking the case), but when he's acting for the wrong reasons, he has the opportunity to grow (and the reader hopes he will).

Next, we always have the option of inducing more sympathy by punishing every good deed. If the character has done the right thing, we can make it backfire—preferably by tying it to the character's bad motivations. So for our character in the above example, when the lawyer takes the case to get closer to the mother, we take him further from that goal. Perhaps the mother is in a relationship with someone else, or she just rejects the lawyer's advances, and fires him from the case just when the case was really starting to get good. As we frustrate his goals, especially as his motivations become better, we increase reader sympathy.

This particular method of establishing character sympathy meshes well with setting up a character arc. When we're able to show that a character's previous motivations and behaviors (preying on client's mothers, or just taking advantage of people in this example) simply aren't a positive way to live, and the character truly needs to grow and change in order to live a happy, fulfilling life, we're effectively setting up a character to go on a journey to make that growth happen.

A second option could be to have the character do the "wrong" thing—make the less sympathetic choice—for the

EFFECTIVE METHODS OF CREATING CHARACTER SYMPATHY

right reasons. Again, this digs deep into the character's motivations, and thus it could be a stronger way to help to create sympathy with the character.

If the character did the wrong thing for the right reasons, we can engineer the consequences of the wrong choice to become even worse. Let's say our lawyer doesn't take the charity case because he knows he couldn't prove the underlying conspiracy theory the defendant is using as a defense.

Our lawyer is still interested in the case and follows the developments. When the only lawyer the defendant can get loses the case, our lawyer really feels bad about his choice. The wrong person is sent to prison and the conspiracy is covered up forever. Now our lawyer regrets his earlier decision—and as the only one who can prove the truth, he really needs to act.

We can make this even worse when the villains discover that the defendant consulted with our lawyer, and they target him next. Now, as the only person who might be able to prove the truth, he's is in danger.

When our character does the right thing without the right motivations, or when he does the wrong thing (even with noble motivations), we give him the opportunity for growth. But first we must show that his decisions or his motivations were wrong, making his journey harder.

The struggle may be the most important part of the "save the cat" principle, not the strength that the character must show in action. The inner conflict the character experiences, especially when acting for complicated reasons, is especially compelling. The struggle and the conflict here come from the *cost* of the character's actions. If there's no risk to him in "saving the cat," if he stands to lose nothing either way, there's not a whole lot for our readers to root for. If instead, the character must sacrifice something personal, the readers can feel more for him. "We may cheer at the moment when a hero defeats a villain," says Donald Maass in *The Breakout Novelist*, "but we are moved far more deeply when that hero makes a tough choice and honors his code" (17). As authors, we can engineer this choice to the greatest effect on our character.

If we're not careful about our characterization and showing his actions, those actions can begin to look like superfluous add-ons designed to manipulate readers. Our goal isn't to manipulate readers but to have our character demonstrate to our readers *why* he deserves to share his story, why he matters. We must make our character's actions that show this organically related to the story and the character.

Environment

External factors also play a big role in creating character sympathy. While it might be easy to veer too much into using setting, for example, to create character sympathy, restraint and calculation can make this a good tool to help convey our character as well as instill the same feelings, emotions and responses in our readers as in our character.

Effective Methods of Creating Character Sympathy

In *How to Write a Damn Good Novel, II,* James N. Frey suggests using the setting to help establish the reader's identification with the character:

> You do it by using the power of suggestion. You use sensuous and emotion-provoking details that suggest to the reader what it is like to be [the character] and to suffer what he is suffering. In other words, you create the story world in such a way that the readers can put themselves in the character's place....
>
> You can win empathy for a character by detailing the sensuous details in the environment: the sights, sounds, pains, smells, and so on that the character is feeling—the feelings that trigger his emotions. (19)

Obviously, this doesn't mean that every sad sack character should be trudging through the pouring rain (to the courthouse to try to win his freedom from a wrongful conviction), much as that might help. We've all seen this done so much that it verges on cliché. Once again, restraint and a careful hand are vital to making this work.

Instead of slathering on the atmospheric effects, we can use the setting to help establish the character's emotional set. Doing this helps to not only ground our story in the physical world and convey the setting to the reader, it helps to do so in a way that creates emotion.

To use the character's environment to effectively

reinforce character sympathy requires that the character first take notice of his environs. Though this may be the five thousandth time he's been in this room, there could still be some telling detail we can use to convey the character's emotional set, whether it's the tired, threadbare chair to the perky pillows perfectly perched on the paisley bedspread. The details that a character notices are always filtered through his interests and personality—and his current emotional state.

Using the setting to reflect and mirror—or possibly contrast or mock—his internal emotional state reinforces this on an almost subconscious level. The reader can't actually see the chair or the pillows, so it's the character's judgment that helps to create the image in their mind. By using emotionally-themed description in establishing the setting, the reader can visualize whatever type of chair or pillows best fit their own perceptions of sadness or happiness, powerfully reinforcing the emotional imagery and helping to create the same emotional response within the reader, the ultimate goal of character sympathy.

Dramatic irony

The physical props in the setting aren't the only ways to use the environment to increase the reader's sympathy with the characters' plight. The time period and the events of the plot can also help readers identify with the characters and their struggles, even if the characters themselves are not yet aware of them.

The technique of making the reader aware of something

that one or more of the characters doesn't know is called dramatic irony. In her article "Subtext: the fourth dimension," author/editor Alicia Rasley points out one excellent example: "Most everyone who saw the film *Casablanca* when it first came out understood the significance of the film's time period—the first few days of December 1941. The characters did not know it, but viewers knew that in less than a week, the neutral United States was going to join the world war."

The principle of dramatic irony doesn't just apply to the historical milieu of the story. We can create our own dramatic irony by informing the audience of coming events. At the beginning of *Romeo and Juliet*, for example, Shakespeare starts off with an ominous prologue, warning against the parents' feud and the terrible fate it will bring. This helps to pique the viewer's interest, pulling them into the conflict that even the characters may not realize is coming. Because the actions on the stage are the only way for Shakespeare to show his characters, he establishes their coming tragedy to help increase reader identification early on.

EFFECTIVE ANTAGONISTS

If we can introduce the antagonist of the story early on, sometimes we can create more sympathy for the main characters by making their opposition even worse. We show the antagonist as stronger or comparatively worse than our main characters, and our readers can root for our characters to defeat these bad guys.

Some antagonist characteristics that can help improve the main characters in the readers' eyes include:

- **Strength**. The antagonist is probably going to be stronger than the protagonist, especially at the beginning of the story. Our character having to face an insurmountable challenge—a struggle—helps the readers to care more about the character.
- **Goals**. The antagonist has a goal that opposes the main character's goals, or worse still, hurts other people.
- **Low value on human life**. In many genres, the antagonists are actually hurting or even killing people.
- **Stakes**. The antagonist poses an immediate threat to the main character or someone s/he cares about.

An effective antagonist helps to give our character conflict and struggles. If our antagonist's most important role in creating character sympathy is to make the hero look good by comparison, however, we should use other methods for creating character sympathy for our hero. The lesser of two evils is still evil, and a book full of people the reader doesn't want to read about is probably not going to get read.

HUMOR

We mentioned in the previous chapter that klutziness, a common source of comedic relief, is not an effective method for establishing character sympathy, partially because it's overused, and partially because it's trying a bit too hard to make the reader *like* the character. Humor, however, can be one tool for creating character sympathy when we use it correctly.

Effective Methods of Creating Character Sympathy

A sense of humor helps to make a character more relatable. It can give the character an air of resilience, which is a strength worth rooting for. Whether the story events are positive or negative for the character, if he can take everything with a joke, he remains more grounded for the reader. Humor helps to temper the extremes of both strength and struggles, and make the character more human. And of course, when our character gets in the perfect one-liner or comeback, the readers (like us) get to indulge in a little wish-fulfillment for all the times words have failed them in a fight.

Several types of humor work particularly well with this, including wit and sarcasm, especially used in a self-deprecating way. Being able to poke fun at herself makes a character more endearing. Making fun of another character in a mean-spirited way, bullying, and cruelty, however, are very likely to backfire on the character-sympathy level.

This tool for creating character sympathy is optional. It's not suited to all characters or all stories. But if your character is struggling to engage your readers, perhaps a joke or two couldn't hurt.

Timing

We most need to create character sympathy comes at the very beginning of the story, where it's make or break for the reader. If we can't capture the readers' interest, and then their hearts through identification, they will not continue reading. As Blake Snyder says in an "adjunct" to his Save the Cat principle, "A screenwriter [and a fiction writer] must be mindful of getting the audience 'in sync' with the plight of the hero from the very start" (121).

Establishing character sympathy early on not only engages our readers, but helps to make them invested in the character's goals. When the reader wants to find out whether the character will attain those goals, the reader keeps reading. And that's exactly what we want.

EXAMPLES OF CHARACTER SYMPATHY

Skillful storytellers weave together the techniques of creating character sympathy to create the best effect.

Sometimes the best way to understand a principle is to see it in action. A concrete, successful pattern can help you see how character sympathy is created, how it works in practice, and how to avoid common pitfalls in character sympathy.

I've selected these examples because they use the techniques we've discussed, while avoiding possible a few of the following examples because they're exceptions to the rules. Examining these unusual characters helps to show us techniques that we can utilize when our own character falls outside the normal parameters used to establish character sympathy.

HARRY POTTER THE SAD SACK

Harry Potter has become one of the most well-loved characters in popular literature today. Anyone familiar with the stories can recount his beginnings: orphaned, left to live with his abusive aunt and uncle, forced to live under the stairs while his pampered cousin continued to be spoiled.

Those characteristics could be enough to begin to push Harry into the realm of the sad sack—but that isn't where the first novel in the series, *Harry Potter and the Philosopher's (Sorcerer's) Stone*, begins. Instead, J.K. Rowling starts with the Dursleys. The omniscient narrator dips into their viewpoints in the first chapter, especially Mr. Dursley's, and uses their own thoughts and opinions to show them as smug, judgmental and superficial, even toward their own kin. They don't see their own rudeness,

CHARACTER SYMPATHY

nosiness, self-satisfaction and coddling of a nascent brat, but the reader can tell these people are no good.

Meanwhile, in the events of the story, Rowling carefully creates suspense about what's to come. With the character's name in the title, the reader knows to be attuned to mentions of him, and there are a few brief allusions before he's finally directly discussed on page twelve. The unusual events occurring—from owls flocking to town to cape-wearing revelers suddenly showing up—keep the reader's attention.

In his first appearance in the novel, Harry is a baby. His parents have just been murdered by a mysterious, evil wizard who is so frightening even other wizards don't dare to utter his name. And yet somehow, the wizard was unable to kill Harry himself, a defenseless baby.

While a reader will have some automatic sympathy (or pity) for an orphaned baby, unfortunately, a baby can't *do* a lot to earn the reader's identification. The second chapter of the book skips a decade to Harry's sad-sack prepubescent existence. Because of the setup in the first chapter, we know that there's something special about Harry, and we get glimpses of that throughout the second chapter, hints of his special powers when his hair magically grows back, or he mystically escapes his cousin's beating, and especially as they're shown when the glass disappears.

Because the reader dislikes the Dursleys so much, their unjust hatred of Harry makes the reader like him more.

The reader sees the injustice in their mistreatment of Harry. When he's able to evade them, even accidentally, the reader cheers for him, ready to join him on his escape from this miserable life when the summons to Hogwarts comes with the big reveal: "You're a wizard, Harry!"

Consider if Dudley Dursley, Harry's cousin, received the notice that he was a wizard instead of Harry. He'd most likely be eager to leave behind the parents that love and pamper him to embark on the new adventure. It seems likely Dudley wouldn't miss his parents (until he was no longer being spoiled), and would leave them behind without a second thought.

If Harry were characterized that way—leaving behind a loving family to go chase adventures—the reader would have much less sympathy for him. Instead, Rowling generates sympathy by making his life horrible, and the reader is onboard with his decision to leave it all behind.

SUPERHEROES, SUPER STRENGTH

No one struggles with strength like superheroes. Their powers are literally superhuman, so they're perfect examples of tempering strengths with struggles.

Superman

Superman is the archetypal superhero. With super strength, super speed, flight, invincibility and other powers, he's set the standard for superhumans.

Character Sympathy

Superman's full arsenal of powers developed over time, as did his origin story—and his weaknesses. Eventually, an invulnerable superhero becomes predictable, even trite.

Interestingly, the voice behind the radio serial is one of the reasons why the creators of Superman had to find a weakness for him. With his popularity, the demand for Superman's voice became too much for voice actor Bud Collyer. To give him a break, the creators found a new weakness for Superman: Kryptonite.

Since its first introduction, the varieties and effects of Kryptonite have only increased. The series writers have found other ways to strip Superman of his strengths, keeping the story interesting and relatable to readers.

Taking away his strength isn't the only way the creators have worked to build his character sympathy. Over time, he developed a strict moral code, placing the highest priority on human life and justice.

But possibly the most effective way Superman gains reader identification is through his secret identity as Clark Kent. Where Superman is strong and confident, Kent is self-effacing and awkward. When well acted, Clark Kent's shyness doesn't just look like Superman pretending to be less than he is. Instead, the viewer has the opportunity to sympathize with his struggles at work and with women. (This is especially true as he tries to win over Lois Lane as Clark Kent instead of Superman.)

Often, Superman "reset" stories focus on these struggles

Examples of Character Sympathy

during his journey of self-discovery, when he learns of his superpowers and his true nature. He's often a gawky teenager during this phase, uncomfortable with his powers and his environment. But as he comes to master his powers, the viewer gets to indulge in wish-fulfillment fantasy as everyman Kent becomes superhero Superman, who is not only superhumanly strong, but also more confident and capable.

Batman

Batman doesn't actually have superpowers: he's a regular person who's developed many, many skills from physical prowess to intelligence to inventing cool gadgets. He can resist mind control and pain, he can escape from any trap, he can disguise himself as almost anyone. He has mastered martial arts, science and law enforcement. If anyone could be too perfect, it could be Batman.

As a comic book character, Batman premiered in May 1939. Six months later, DC Comics (then National Publications) printed his origin story, where his parents are murdered in front of him as a child, and he vows vengeance upon all criminals. Even his sidekick, Robin, is an orphan. This is of course the tragic backstory technique that's become so clichéd in the last seventy-five years.

The tragic backstory sets up Batman's motivations, but it isn't the only reason readers are supposed to sympathize with him. We often get to see him sacrificing his personal life to fight crime—it often seems Batman is the real

Character Sympathy

person and Bruce Wayne is the mask. He fights crime with little thanks much of the time. As a vigilante, he's not really aligned with the police, and they also make his life more difficult.

Some argue that Batman's humanity and his moral code are his greatest weaknesses. Although the original character was often ruthless, Batman evolved over time into someone unwilling to sacrifice innocent people in pursuit of justice. His reluctance to take even a villain's life is often a disadvantage to him. But showing his moral code and his high value of human life helps to generate more sympathy for him, especially when this moral code makes things more difficult for him, but he does what's right anyway.

As with many superheroes, a villain discovering his "real" identity is always a potential vulnerability. Finally, the simple fact that he *doesn't* have superpowers is a weakness for Batman. Without superstrength or regenerating powers, he's ultimately susceptible to the same injuries any other human might be.

That humanity is possibly one of the greatest reasons why readers and viewers sympathize with Batman. Despite his unrealistic laundry list of strengths, readers see that he's a regular human, and readers *could* become like him. For a character as skilled as Batman, emphasizing his humanity can help readers relate to him better.

Spy Another Day—Sacrifice for Sympathy

In my own works, I (usually) make a conscious effort to create character sympathy for my main character. In my Spy Another Day series, I utilized several techniques in each book to help readers identify with my main character. "Save the cat!" moments of sacrifice and putting someone else's needs first have featured prominently in a couple of the books.

In *I, Spy*, I open with the a scene of the character, Talia Reynolds, showing strength and skill in her job as a spy. That doesn't mean everything goes perfectly in her spy mission—she struggles when her coworker's mistake nearly gets her caught. Because of their friendship and long history, she forgives him for his mistakes, and in the next chapter, when his job is on the line, Talia does everything she can to help him. Finally, she strikes a bargain with her boss: if her friend makes another mistake, she'll take the consequences (and the risk). She makes a sacrifice for someone else in a "Save the coworker!" moment.

In *Spy for a Spy*, I again open with a scene of Talia showing strength and skill as a spy. Nothing ever goes smoothly for a spy, so there are challenges. But her real struggles don't start until the end of the chapter, when she arrives back at her office to meet her new boss: her ex-boyfriend.

I couldn't stop there, however. I didn't want to give away exactly how badly their relationship ended at the beginning of the book, so I turned to the pattern of Scarlett O'Hara's first encounter with Rhett Butler for more help. Talia's ex-boyfriend makes fun of her, but she's able to respond in kind. But then he insults her, and his taunting cuts right to her heart, not only embarrassing her, but making her doubt herself.

In the forthcoming final novel, *Tomorrow We Spy*, I almost forgot to create character sympathy! Fortunately, my wonderful critique partners not only called me on my slip, but came up with great ideas on what I could do to help make Talia worthy of reader identification again.

In the current version, she's finally let her guard down, away from her job as a spy and on her honeymoon. When someone suspicious tracks her down, she tries to get rid of him, showing strength—but when he pursues their innocent old landlady, Talia must decide whether to stay with her husband or go after the landlady to draw away the pursuer and keep her safe. The inner conflict is a struggle for Talia, but she ultimately makes a sacrifice to protect someone else.

ROMEO AND JULIET AND DRAMATIC IRONY

In a romance, we often have two main characters to build sympathy for. In the epitome of romantic tragedy, Shakespeare carefully builds sympathy for Romeo and Juliet's plight by first showing their situation so that the viewer can understand the challenge they face.

First, the prologue sets an ominous tone for the "star-

Examples of Character Sympathy

cross'd lovers." This creates dramatic irony, cueing the viewer into the significance of the events to follow, which is good, because neither of those lovers appears when the action begins. Instead, we begin with their servants and family members feuding in the street. Clever wordplay here also helps to keep viewers' interest until the actual brawl begins. Even Romeo's and Juliet's parents are nearly drawn into the fray before the prince of Verona marches in and breaks up the fight.

Finally, Romeo arrives on the scene—mooning over another girl. However, he's been unlucky in love this time, and he's very heartsick, though he keeps up the witty banter with his cousin. The viewer quickly sees his strength in wit and in devotion, and struggles with unrequited love.

In the second scene, we learn that Count Paris is seeking Juliet's hand in marriage even though she's not quite fourteen.

The first two scenes (about a sixth of the play) are spent building the conflict between the two families, establishing the hopeless situation Romeo and Juliet face. When Juliet is finally introduced, she has very few lines in her first scene. Instead, her nursemaid prattles on while Lady Capulet tries to talk to her daughter. Juliet is the one who silences her nurse, showing strength which even her mother doesn't possess. When Lady Capulet conveys Paris's proposal, Juliet dutifully agrees to consider him at the party that night, again demonstrating strength in her devotion to her mother. Her struggles are more implied:

Character Sympathy

she's powerless to guide her own fate. However, her willingness to sacrifice her future in filial piety demonstrates a form of the "save the cat" moment.

Shakespeare also draws on the power of dramatic irony to convey his characters' ultimate struggle, against their family's feud. The viewer becomes invested in this feud as the young couple meets and falls in love, a love that's stronger and purer than any other they've experienced. The viewer roots for the characters to succeed against all odds and all information they've received about the setting and situation.

Of course in a tragedy, the characters ultimately fail in their quest, but the journey and the lessons learn help viewers find catharsis. But to achieve that emotional release, we must first engage our readers' emotions by creating that identification.

Arabian Nights and Putting It All Together

The way we portray our characters makes all the difference in developing reader sympathy. Consider this version of the popular story from the *Arabian Nights*:

> Once upon a time, there was a young man who was a habitual thief. Even though his family was perfectly capable of providing for him, and even though he was perfectly capable of working to support himself, he stole everything he owned and stole from anyone

Examples of Character Sympathy

> could. He even subjugated innocent animals to make them steal for him.
>
> In the same kingdom, there was a beautiful princess. Rich, powerful, handsome, kind men traveled from all over the world at the mere hope of winning her hand. Her doting father gave her everything she could ever want, and all he asked was that she marry, so that he could rest assured that she would be taken care of when he was gone. (Well, okay, he also would have liked to play with his grandkids before he went, too.) But the princess spurned and humiliated every suitor that came her way and simply refused to marry.

We can't wait for these two to get together for their happily ever after, right? Of course not. Right away, the reader is turned off by the characters and their motivations and actions.

The Walt Disney animators are much more savvy than that. They use the same basic setup of the story, but they make sure to include several details, characteristics and actions to help viewers support and sympathize with characters that are doing less than desirable things.

In Disney's *Aladdin*, they spent the first several minutes setting up the characters and the plot to make them more likeable:
- Dramatic irony: the movies starts with a framing story to set up how important the hero is, how legendary he

is, and hint that great things will happen to this "diamond in the rough."

- Struggle: he steals out of necessity. He's an orphan, and he has to steal to eat.
- Struggle: he is persecuted. The city's guards catch him stealing quite regularly and chase him through the streets.
- Strength: he is smart and charming, and evades the guards through trickery.
- Sacrifice: after working hard to get away with a single loaf of bread (and sharing with his animal sidekick), when he sees two hungry orphans he gives them his whole meal. Yes, we're actually using the cliché of helping orphans, but not to flaunt the character's strength. Helping fellow orphans here comes with personal cost. He doesn't just write a check from his trust fund—he gives up the meal he just fought for. He will go hungry, and it will probably take great risk and effort to eat again.
- Struggle & strength: a rich, haughty guy tries to tell our hero off completely without justification, and the crowd laughs. But our hero will have none of that and throws haughty guy's words back in his face.
- Struggles: But the rich, haughty guy gets the last word—he says to our hero, "You are a worthless street rat. You were born a street rat, you'll die a street rat, and only your fleas will mourn you." Then the palace doors slam shut, making sure our hero can't retort and reinforcing just how destitute he is—and in his heart of hearts, we can see he's worried that the rich,

Examples of Character Sympathy

haughty guy is right. (Very like Scarlett.)

That's within the first seven or eight minutes (and I didn't even mention how he saved the orphans' lives). The heroine, of course, wants to marry for love, and all her suitors are only interested in power and money. Her father could easily be cast as a bad guy—the evil tyrant forcing her to marry against her will—but in this treatment, he keeps those nice sentiments that we gave him before.

The storytellers at Disney successfully weave together the techniques of character sympathy to get viewers on board with a character who could have easily been very unsympathetic.

Prickly Characters

Some iconic characters that are well loved don't develop character sympathy in conventional ways—but without that sympathy, their stories wouldn't have survived through the years.

Ebenezer Scrooge

Ebenezer Scrooge is such an iconic character that his name has become synonymous with misers. He's an interesting character study in creating character sympathy because he is a very unlikeable character at first, setting himself up for an impressive reversal through his character arc.

In *How to Write a Damn Good Novel*, James N. Frey

Character Sympathy

describes the way that Charles Dickens built Ebenezer Scrooge's reader identification, following Frey's model. First, he raises creates an emotion in the reader. Normally, these emotions are positive, but for Scrooge, Frey says, that emotion is contempt (111).

Then, Frey says, he's thrown into a series of escalating conflicts. In the opening of *A Christmas Carol*, those conflicts begin with a visit from Scrooge's nephew, then two men collecting donations for the poor, culminating with visitations from the spirits of Marley, and then Christmases past, present and future.

However, I think there's one more essential, subtle step in these first conflicts, a step that sets up the character arc:

> "Christmas a humbug, uncle!" said Scrooge's nephew. "You don't mean that, I am sure."
> "I do," said Scrooge. "Merry Christmas! What right have you to be merry? what reason have you to be merry? You're poor enough."
> "Come, then," returned the nephew gaily. "What right have you to be dismal? what reason have you to be morose? You're rich enough."
> Scrooge having no better answer ready on the spur of the moment, said, "Bah!" again; and followed it up with "Humbug."

Scrooge has lived his life believing that money could bring him happiness, which is why he's so miserly. However, his nephew points out that Scrooge *isn't* happy, that his worldview is based on a false belief.

Examples of Character Sympathy

Not only does this show the reader that Scrooge has room to grow, and he knows it, the scene also does so in such a way that the reader almost feels for Scrooge as his nephew gets the best of him, even though the nephew is obviously right. While readers may not start off seeing themselves in Scrooge, but this gives a glimpse of how much Scrooge subconsciously needs the change, which helps the readers to root for that change.

Sherlock Holmes

Sherlock Holmes is another iconic character, but after more than a century of popularity, our view of the world's greatest detective has definitely become romanticized. We quickly forget his detached nature, how little he cares for most people around him, living instead for the thrill of the Game.

So how did Sir Arthur Conan Doyle create sympathy for Holmes? First, he didn't—remember that Watson is the first-person narrator of virtually all Sherlock Holmes stories. The first Sherlock Holmes story, *A Study in Scarlet*, begins by introducing Watson and his service in the Afghan War. Rather than making him a war hero, however, as Watson says, "The campaign brought honours and promotion to many, but for me it had nothing but misfortune and disaster." He is injured, and then takes sick until he has to return to England, where he has a small pension and lives alone.

Watson has the struggles covered, obviously. His strength

Character Sympathy

comes in his indomitable character. He does bemoan his troubles in the war, but he describes himself "as free as air" upon his return to London.

When he runs into an acquaintance from medical school, he's so happy to see a familiar face, he treats him like an old friend. This friend, Stamford, mentions that he knows someone else looking for a room. Watson latches onto the idea, but Stamford warns him: "You don't know Sherlock Holmes yet. . . . perhaps you would not care for him as a constant companion."

As is only appropriate for the greatest fictional detective ever, the reader's first contact with Sherlock Holmes is mysterious. Stamford describes his strange studies and habits—from chemical studies to beating dead bodies—but doesn't know *why* Holmes studies all these fields, piquing the reader's curiosity further.

The reader first meets Holmes at the moment of discovering a new reagent that reacts only with blood, a major triumph for him and criminal investigation. He shows high intelligence—and he instantly deduces Watson's war history, though he doesn't explain that deduction, increasing the mystery. Holmes's strengths are quickly on display.

Stamford mentioned some of Holmes's odd proclivities before, but Holmes is straightforward about them, inventorying his vices to determine if he and Watson will make good roommates. He lists his pipe and chemicals, and continues:

Examples of Character Sympathy

> Let me see—what are my other shortcomings. I get in the dumps at times, and don't open my mouth for days on end. You must not think I am sulky when I do that. Just let me alone, and I'll soon be right. What have you to confess now? It's just as well for two fellows to know the worst of one another before they begin to live together.

Paired with Stamford's information about Holmes, this list hints at his struggles: Holmes's weakness is often interpersonal skills. He's capricious and sometimes inconsiderate while in pursuit of a case.

Once they've agreed to be roommates, Watson leaves with Stamford again, and his friend gives him an assignment: "You must study him, then. . . . You'll find him a knotty problem, though. I'll wager he learns more about you than you about him." Watson, and the reader, are intrigued enough to take that wager, and the study begins.

It's significant that Holmes is not the narrator. While he's an interesting character to study from a distance, it would be much more difficult for the reader to identify with someone whose primary concern is the abstract pursuit of knowledge and mental stimulation to escape the burden of his intellectual speed. Instead, using Watson as a surrogate, the reader can be intrigued by Holmes instead of being frustrated and disgusted by him.

Sympathy for Other Characters

Most of our efforts in generating character sympathy rightly focus on the main character, the protagonist. However, he isn't the only one who can benefit from reader identification.

LOVE INTEREST SYMPATHY

Often, the love interest in a story will be a main character, or even have a viewpoint and narrate scenes. When the love interest plays such a central role, he will have enough "screen" time to build sympathy like any other main character.

Sometimes, however, the love interest doesn't have a viewpoint or enough "screen" time to create reader identification like a main character. In these cases, we must be careful about how we present the love interest, and how the main character perceives the love interest, as these are the key ways the reader comes to know him.

Be careful to avoid accidentally characterizing the love interest as unsympathetic. Watch out for actions that might undermine readers' sympathy. Even if the heroine believes she can rescue him from his self-destructive or dangerous behaviors, if the readers don't want the love interest to be rescued, her savior complex will undermine reader identification with her as well.

That isn't to say the love interest has to be a paragon of perfection every minute he's on the page. Often the hero and heroine are in conflict, and may be an antagonist to one another's goals. When this is the case, it's especially important to make the love interest's goals and motivations clear. Why does he not want her to open a coffee shop there? His motivation might be selfless—he's afraid failure will crush her soul. Or he might be selfishly motivated—he owns the nearest Starbucks.

Selfless motivations generally work better when the love interest knows the main character well and they already have a close, if not romantic, relationship. A virtual stranger who worries about our heroine's soul being crushed seems a bit odd and unrealistic. Selfish motivations, on the other hand, can work for any setup—but obviously a selfish motivation isn't the best way to get a reader on board.

When using selfish motivations, then, it becomes even more important to build sympathy. One of the surest ways to do this is to use the "save the cat" moment, where the character helps someone else, especially if they must sacrifice to do so. A selfless act like this is especially important when the character's motivations for opposing our protagonist are selfish.

These selfish motivations may set up a character arc for the love interest, wherein he learns the error of his ways, and we'll rely on other techniques to build his sympathy. But when his selfish motivations aren't "wrong" in that way, we can help keep his portrayal sympathetic by showing his noble reasons for the selfish motivation.

In this selfish motivation example, the love interest opposes the heroine's coffee shop development because he owns a Starbucks nearby. If he's supposed to grow in a character arc, he may be motivated by pure avarice (and we'll have to create sympathy in other ways). However, if he isn't supposed to embark on a journey of emotional growth, we must show readers that he's still worthy of their identification by showing the noble reasons behind that selfish motivation. Perhaps he's a single dad and the Starbucks is supporting his family. To dig even deeper in sympathy, maybe he's even had the same dream as the heroine, starting a mom-and-pop neighborhood coffee shop. He couldn't take the risk himself, so the heroine's plan reminds him of how he sold out his own dream for security.

SECONDARY CHARACTER SYMPATHY

Sympathy is not quite as vital for secondary characters, but sometimes it's crucial that a secondary character have reader sympathy to help the overall narrative.

In general, a secondary character's need for sympathy is proportional to their role in the story—the more important the character is to the story, the more important it is to establish reader identification with him.

For example, in my novel *I, Spy*, the main character's sympathy largely hinged upon the "Save the cat!" moment of sacrificing herself for her friend and coworker, who made a mistake and endangered her. This was somewhat problematic in early drafts because the friend/coworker looked like an incompetent and unsympathetic sad sack, making the main character's sacrifice look less noble and more unintelligent.

The friend/coworker was vital to the story itself, and also to the main character's sympathy, so I needed to increase his sympathy with the reader.
- I gave him a noble goal—supporting his pregnant

wife—to explain his (recently acquired) incompetence.
- I made him funny. He acquired a flirtatious swagger.
- I carefully tailored how the main character saw him, emphasizing his previous competence, and the sacrifices he'd made for her in the past.

Note that some of those techniques rely on past events to help convey sympathy. We've established that backstory, for example, is never as effective as the current story in affecting reader identification. However, because their "screen" time is so limited, and because their reader identification isn't *as* vital to the story as a whole, occasionally, shortcuts can be useful in establishing sympathy with secondary characters—but these shortcuts can't be the only way we build identification, even for secondaries.

SYMPATHY FOR THE DEVIL: VILLAIN AND ANTAGONIST SYMPATHY

Heroes aren't the only ones who deserve sympathy. While it may not always be strictly necessary, villains and antagonists can benefit from reader identification as well.

Villain sympathy is another common place where a tragic backstory is supposed to help round the characters and create reader identification. However, just as with main characters, villains can't generate true sympathy with sob stories about their sad childhoods.

We want our villains and antagonists to be well-rounded

SYMPATHY FOR OTHER CHARACTERS

characters as well, not flat stereotypes. Generating reader sympathy is a good way to achieve this. Author K.M. Weiland suggests using a "mushy moment" to humanize our antagonist, and she uses the example of the wicked stepmother in the film *Ever After*, an adaptation of the Cinderella story:

> For the only time in the entire movie, [protagonist Danielle and the wicked stepmother] share an interlude in which the stepmother gives Danielle some good, if still snarky, advice ("We mustn't feel sorry for ourselves, must we? No matter how bad things are, they can always get worse!"), then falls into a melancholy reflection of her own plight in having to marry Danielle's father, a man she "hardly knew," who then promptly died on her.

Weiland notes that "The stepmother is as wicked as ever throughout this scene," still maintaining her cruel mistreatment of her stepdaughter and forcing her to do menial labor for her. Clearly, the intention of the scene is not to make the viewer love or even like the stepmother. Weiland concludes:

> But in the way in which the dialogue is spoken, [the director] makes her real. We understand that the stepmother's nastiness, if only in this scene, is a defensive mechanism to cover up her own pains and fears. Even if we can't condone her horridness, we are at least given an opportunity to understand it. Every antagonist deserves that much.

Rather than piling on tragedy after tragedy in the character's past, this single "mushy" moment helps to

Character Sympathy

show the villain's humanity in the present story by focusing on the emotional impact of the past events. If we can do this while maintaining the character's negative portrayal, as in this example, it hammers that home to the reader even more.

There's a delicate balance to strike here. Too much focus on making your reader sympathize with your villain can backfire: if the reader identifies with the villain more than the hero, they may not root for the hero to ultimately win anymore. Relying on a brief moment to show the villain's vulnerabilities, his or her weaknesses, helps to strike that balance. We're not trying to get the reader to support the villain's ultimate goal necessarily, simply to see the antagonist as human for even one brief scene.

In stories with character arcs, this "mushy" moment can also help to show that the antagonist is struggling with the same (or the opposite) mistaken beliefs about the world and himself that the protagonist is. It's the protagonist's growth of journey throughout the course of the story that helps her to make the ultimate choice to grow beyond the point where the antagonist stagnates and stews in this broken belief. Thus, the protagonist becomes stronger than the antagonist, and she can ultimately defeat him.

Villains aren't the only ones who face challenges to their sympathy. Even after we've worked to create character sympathy, our heroes might still lose that reader identification if we're not careful.

Common Challenges to Character Sympathy

Even the most unlovable character can generate reader identification. However, these characters are such a special case that they warrant further discussion.

UNLOVABLE CHARACTERS

Because our character begins in a position where he needs to grow, he sometimes has a lot of flaws at the outset. He can be so flawed that he becomes almost unlovable.

Sometimes we believe our character is so bad, so prickly, so off-putting to the reader, the reader can't identify with him. If our characters make Oscar the Grouch look like Guy Smiley, we face a big challenge in getting the reader to identify with them. The reader needs to see the character struggling, to witness the inner conflict. Perhaps he isn't "conflicted" about his grouchy nature in the beginning—Ebenezer Scrooge certainly isn't openly conflicted about his miserliness. In that case, it's less inner conflict and more making it painfully obvious to the reader that the character's attitudes and beliefs cannot produce his ultimate fulfillment. Scrooge is not on a path to happiness at the outset, even though he can't see that yet.

The reader also needs to have some hope the character can change. Let the readers think for even a minute that the character is going through that inner struggle. Give the character a moment of self-doubt, where she looks over all the relationships she's broken and wonder, even for a minute, if this unfortunate circumstance is all of her own making.

Even if that moment only lasts that long, the reader has the opportunity to see that the character is capable of growth. She *can* see that their situation is bad, and that could be the first step toward making it better.

And what about those characters who *aren't* going to make it better? We have a term for them: antiheroes.

Antiheroes

Some heroes have more in common with other stories' villains. An antihero will do the wrong thing even if he knows it's wrong, and he isn't on a journey to become a better person.

Editor Theresa Stevens argues that we should set up an antihero in much the same way we would a hero: we foster character sympathy with strengths, struggles, noble goals and inner conflict. However, instead of showing a flawed character who needs to grow, and might have the capacity to do so, with an antihero, Stevens says, "There must be suggestions of bad behavior we can expect in the future, hints and innuendos and even outright badness—foreshadowing, if you will. In other words, you have to provide a suggestion that there is badness in the character, but that suggestion must not be strong enough to overpower the character's initial likability" ("Introducing an Antihero: Big Good, Little Bad"). (Note that actually being likeable may be an important part of an antihero.)

An important distinction to make here is that these are not tragic heroes. Their "badness" will not result in their ultimate failure. Instead, the work serves as almost a psychological profile of someone who behaves so radically differently that it's fascinating to watch. It can be difficult to pull off, but you can have readers rooting for the most self-destructive, stunted characters even if they never grow.

To do this, we must start by looking to Stevens's definition of an antihero: "An antihero is a character in the role of the protagonist whose actions are villainous but whose motivation makes it tolerable to the reader" ("A Potential Definition of Antihero"). In another article on the topic, "Introducing an Antihero: Big Good, Little Bad," Stevens uses the example of *The Godfather* and Don Corleone. This mob boss certainly does bad things, but his love of his family is a major motivating factor—hence opening the story at Connie's wedding. Antiheroes do bad things for the right reasons, and when the readers see these motivations, they root for the character.

Keeping Character Sympathy

Establishing character sympathy isn't automatic—and neither is keeping it.

Once we've worked so hard to properly establish character sympathy, we must work to keep it, too. But that doesn't mean our character must walk on eggshells or a tightrope of perfection so our readers will always love everything he does. There are certain actions and attributes that we *should* avoid, but for the host of other actions, we must simply be careful about how we portray the character and those choices to keep our readers sympathetic.

USING THE CHARACTER ARC

A character's arc, their journey to internal growth, is one of the most effective ways to draw our readers in and invest them in the character's full journey. Although character arcs are a subject that merit a book of their own, the fundamentals intersect with character sympathy in this area.

The basic principles of character arcs establish a flaw, a need or a wound in the character that needs to be resolved through her emotional growth. When she acts out of the wrong motivations or a mistaken belief about the world, bad things happen. These bad events can help establish sympathy. Continuing along the path of growth produces more struggles, keeping character sympathy, especially as the character slowly learns and grows. Through this model, the greatest reader identification occurs at the climax, the character's ultimate moment of growth.

For more about character arcs, be sure to check out my book *Character Arcs: Founding, forming and finishing*

Character Sympathy

your character's internal journey.

Defeat versus failure

Along the journey of growth, or when facing off with a stronger antagonist, our character will fail from time to time. It's an important part of the learning process. While this pattern is also a good way to keep reader sympathy, it can backfire if our character loses heart early on in the story.

The reader may feel pity for a little while, but it's very difficult to truly root for someone whom they pity. Pity carries an additional element of defeat. If the character not only fails, but allows herself to be defeated, to give up all hope, she's at risk of playing the victim or falling into sad sack territory, and losing reader identification. Failure is a necessary part of life, real and fictional, but defeat is optional.

Actions to avoid

Sometimes it's the character's overt actions that lose reader identification. We're all familiar with the stereotypical character in a horror movie who knows a serial killer is loose and goes running directly into harm's way. Often these characters are derided as "Too Stupid Too Live"—because their own ridiculous actions lead to their death.

Make sure your characters deserve to stay alive, on the pages of the story and in your readers' hearts, by avoiding these actions.

However, sometimes, the character's bad choices aren't just sins of omission. Sometimes we really need our characters to do the wrong thing.

WHEN THE CHARACTER MUST DO SOMETHING BAD

Sometimes, for the sake of plot and character development, the character must do things that aren't sympathetic, or even acceptable to the average reader—or sometimes our character just behaves badly. Our character doesn't have to be a saint to keep character sympathy—but we must be careful how we handle actions that would look objectionable on the surface.

Clear motivations

Often the problem in losing sympathy when the character behaves badly is extremely simple: we've neglected to explain our character's motivations sufficiently. It's very hard for readers to get and stay on board with a character whose actions they simply do not understand. To use an earlier example, if our lawyer character rejected the charity case without any reasoning, he runs the risk of looking more like a villain or an unsympathetic antihero.

If multiple critique partners and beta readers balk at a character's actions, take a look at his motivations. Chances are these motivations have some problems. Perhaps the motivations just need to be clearer, because you haven't sufficiently explained why the character is doing this. On the other hand, maybe you've explained the character's motivations well, but the problem is with the motivations themselves—perhaps the motivations are inherently offensive, or insufficient for the action, or not directly related enough to the action.

The solution, of course, is to clarify and fine-tune the motivations to suit the character's actions so that they make sense to the reader. Because this is so subjective and individualized, often the best way to figure out what problems you need to address here are to turn to readers, possibly even the same readers who diagnosed the problems in the first place.

Motivations and backstory

We've already established that backstory is not a compelling way to create character sympathy for a number of reasons. However, backstory can be much more effectively used to explain the motivations behind specific actions (rather than to excuse the general nature of the character). However, conveying that backstory is still a trick—and sometimes backstory isn't the best way to show motivation at all.

As with characterization, backstory can't be the only way we show a character's motivations. We've mentioned before that relying solely on backstory suggests that we're not just products of our past experiences, but that we're trapped by them. In the world of fiction, this is unfortunately not very compelling. Imagine a character who only ever acts based on the fact that his mother

Keeping Character Sympathy

yelled at him.

That backstory—and the motivation it creates—is probably not going to offer enough internal motivation and conflict to craft a novel around. The only deep conflict in the present that backstory produces is whether the character can escape the past. Unless we can establish stakes for escaping the past in the present story (his marriage will fail if he can't let go of his memories of his mother, for example), the inner conflict and possibly the external conflict are static.

Instead, we should look to the story present as well as backstory to create motivation and conflict.

Backstory is important because it can explain objectionable actions (which are great for increasing reader curiosity), and it gives our characters a place to grow from. But it shouldn't be the only way we motivate our characters—and as our characters grow, their motivations (and actions) will grow and change with them. As editor Theresa Stevens has said:

> Beware the backstory used to shore up character motivations. It often points to a lack of real conflict or to other plot problems. Every time you're tempted to reach backwards to explain why characters are behaving a certain way, stop. Ask yourself if you can fix it in the present story moment, because this will almost always be the stronger fix.

This is one of those instances where backstory can be just a little too convenient, as if we're thinking *I need the characters to argue here so . . . let's give one of them a traumatic event in childhood. (Thanks, Freud.)* Instead, perhaps we should take a longer look at our characters to see if we can't give them a better reason for conflict in the present.

Humanizing bad actions

Sometimes, however, our character's objectionable actions are just plain bad things to do, no matter what their reasons. In these cases, we need to reemphasize the character's humanity in some way to keep our readers in sync with him.

One way to do this is to create high human worth, to borrow the phrase from Donald Maass. Early on, we must show that the character herself places a high value on human life. She cares about others, and she's willing to fight to save someone from a terrible fate. The opposite of this is someone who sees others as only tools for furthering her own purposes.

One famous example of this might be Sherlock Holmes. In both the classic Sir Arthur Conan Doyle originals and Steven Moffat and Mark Gatiss's newest television adaptation, Sherlock is more interested in figuring out puzzles than furthering justice or saving the wrongly accused. He's no Perry Mason; he needs the mental stimulation his cases provide. However, Doyle (and Moffat and Gatiss) manage to generate some sympathy for

Keeping Character Sympathy

him simply by having him help these people, and by having him despise popular attention for his efforts—they're purely a mental pursuit, not for fame or glory.

When we've established that a character values human life, we have a little more leeway in their actions, especially if we can reinforce that value. Sometimes we have to rely on other options. An effective (and comparatively worse) antagonist and a noble goal are often good techniques to lessen the negative impact on the reader of a protagonist's negative action.

Finally, we can also back the character into a corner, forcing him to do something bad. Once again, we must make his motivations clear here so the reader can sympathize. With the right motivations and inner conflict, we can make an action that might cost us reader identification into a struggle that helps increase character sympathy.

As always, these acts must be shown happening on the "screen" of our story to truly impact reader sympathy. Whether we use relative badness, a noble goal or showing motivations to keep our readers engaged, we must be cognizant of actions that might break the spell of reader identification if we want to keep our readers rooting for our character.

Concluding on Character Sympathy

Character sympathy seems automatic. We expect our readers to jump on board with our character right away. But it isn't that simple. When we neglect to create character sympathy, we discover our readers can't relate to our character.

Character sympathy is the foundation for readable fiction. Whether we hope to enlighten or entertain with our writing, we need character sympathy to draw our readers in, and get them to support our character's goals.

This reader identification is established through very careful effort from the writer. With attention to the techniques of struggles, strength, and sacrifice, you can make even the most unlovable character someone your readers can root for.

References

Works Cited

Frey, James N. *How to Write a Damn Good Novel, II: Advanced Techniques for Dramatic Storytelling.* New York, NY: St. Martin's, 1994.

Frey, James N. *How to Write a Damn Good Novel.* New York: St. Martin's, 1987.

Maass, Donald. *The Breakout Novelist: Craft and Strategies for Career Fiction Writers.* Cincinnati, OH: Writer's Digest, 2010.

Mystery Man on Film (Pseudonymous). "The "Raiders" Story Conference." *Mystery Man on Film.* 9 Mar. 2009. <http://mysterymanonfilm.blogspot.com/2009/03/raiders-story-conference.html>.

Rasley, Alicia. "Subtext: The Fourth Dimension." *AliciaRasley.com.* 2004. <http://www.aliciarasley.com/artsubtext.htm>.

Rasley, Alicia. "Sympathy without Saintliness." *AliciaRasley.com.* 2003. <http://www.aliciarasley.com/artsympathy.htm>.

Snyder, Blake. *Save the Cat!: The Last Book on Screenwriting You'll Ever Need.* Studio City, CA: M. Wiese Productions, 2005.

Stevens, Theresa. "Got Backstory? What Do You Do With It?" *Romance University.* 22 May 2009. <http://romanceuniversity.org/2009/05/22/got-backstory-what-do-you-do-with-it/>.

Stevens, Theresa. "Introducing an Antihero: Big Good, Little Bad." *Edittorrent.* 26 July 2008. <http://edittorrent.blogspot.com/2008/07/introducing-antihero-big-good-little.html>.

Stevens, Theresa. "A Potential Definition of Antihero." *Edittorrent.* 12 July 2008. <http://edittorrent.blogspot.com/2008/07/potential-definition-of-antihero.html>.

Weiland, K.M. "Why Your Antagonist Needs a Mushy Moment." *Helping Writers Become Authors.* 19 Feb. 2014. <http://www.helpingwritersbecomeauthors.com/2014/02/antagonist-needs-mushy-moment.html>.

EXAMPLES CITED

Aladdin. Dir. John Musker and Ron Clements. Perf. Linda Larkin and Scott Weinger. Buena Vista Pictures Distribution, Inc., 1992.

References

Casablanca. Dir. Michael Curtiz. Perf. Humphrey Bogart and Ingrid Bergman. Warner Bros., 1942.

Dickens, Charles. *A Christmas Carol*.

Doyle, Arthur Conan. *A Study in Scarlet*.

Ever After. Dir. Andy Tennant. By Susannah Grant and Rick Parks. Perf. Drew Barrymore, Anjelica Huston, and Dougray Scott. Twentieth Century Fox, 1998.

Frozen. Dir. Jennifer Lee and Chris Buck. Perf. Idina Menzel and Kristen Bell. Walt Disney Pictures, 2013.

The Godfather. Dir. Francis Ford Coppola. By Mario Puzo, Gordon Willis, William Reynolds, Peter Zinner, and Nino Rota. Perf. Marlon Brando, Al Pacino, James Caan. Paramount Pictures, 1972.

One Thousand and One Arabian Nights.

McCollum, Jordan. *I, Spy*. Pleasant Grove, Utah: Durham Crest, 2013.

McCollum, Jordan. *Spy for a Spy*. Pleasant Grove, Utah: Durham Crest, 2013.

McCollum, Jordan. *Tomorrow We Spy*. Pleasant Grove, Utah: Durham Crest, 2014 (forthcoming).

Mitchell, Margaret. *Gone with the Wind*. New York: Macmillan, 1936.

Phineas and Ferb. Dirs. Dan Povenmire and Jeff Marsh. Television.

The Raiders of the Lost Ark. Dir. Steven Spielberg. Perf. Harrison Ford and Karen Allen. Paramount, 1981.

Rowling, J. K. *Harry Potter and the Philosopher's Stone*. London: Bloomsbury, 1997.

Shakespeare, William. *Romeo and Juliet*.

FURTHER READING

A few selected resources I think are especially helpful in creating character sympathy.

Hardy, Janice. "So What? Making Readers Care." *Fiction University*. 11 Apr. 2011. <http://blog.janicehardy.com/2009/07/why-should-i-care.html>.

Hardy, Janice. "What's My Motivation? Tips on Showing Character Motivations." *Fiction University*. 23 Mar. 2012. <http://blog.janicehardy.com/2012/03/whats-my-motivation-tips-on-showing.html>.

Larkin, C. S. "Resonating with Both Classic Heroes and Dark Protagonists." *Live Write Thrive*. 5 Mar. 2014. <http://www.livewritethrive.com/2014/03/05/resonating-with-both-classic-heroes-and-dark-protagonists/>.

References

Loren, Roni. "Like Me! - How to Create Sympathetic Characters." *RoniLoren.com*. 13 Apr. 2012. <http://www.roniloren.com/blog/2012/4/13/like-me-how-to-create-sympathetic-characters-atozchallenge.html>.

McCollum, Jordan. *Character Arcs: Founding, Forming and Finishing Your Character's Internal Journey*. Pleasant Grove, Utah: Durham Crest, 2013.

Mooderino (Pseudonymous). "Forcing Readers To Like Characters." *MOODY WRITING*. 10 Jan. 2013. <http://moodywriting.blogspot.co.uk/2013/01/forcing-readers-to-like-characters.html>.

Rasley, Alicia. "Character Motivation." *AliciaRasley.com*. 2000. <http://www.aliciarasley.com/artmotive.htm>.

Rasley, Alicia. "Coherence in Backstory." *Edittorrent*. 25 Aug. 2010. <http://edittorrent.blogspot.com/2010/08/coherence-in-backstory.html>.

Rasley, Alicia. "Mulling Character Appeal-- Always Dangerous." *Edittorrent*. 22 Aug. 2010. <http://edittorrent.blogspot.com/2010/08/mulling-character-appeal-always.html>.

Wright, Julie. "The Unloveable Character." *Writing on the Wall*. 12 May 2009. <http://writingonthewallblog.blogspot.com/2009/05/by-julie-wright-i-have-confession-to.html>.

INDEX

A
Aladdin, 60
antagonist, 42, 72
  characteristics, 42
antihero
  definition, 81
antiheroes, 80
Arabian Nights, 59

B
backstory, 9
  and motivation, 88
Batman, 53
beauty, 5
Breakout Novelist, The, 33

C
Casablanca, 41
character arc
  and antagonist, 74
  and motivation, 70
  and motivations, 37
  keeping sympathy, 85
  perfect characters, 2
character sympathy
  definition, ix
Christmas Carol, A, 62
Clark Kent, 52
Conan Doyle, Arthur, 64

D E
defeat, 86
dramatic irony, 41
  example, 57
Ebenezer Scrooge, 62, 79
Eeyore, 3
emotions
  provoking readers', 17
environment, 39
Ever After, 73

F
failure, 86
Frey, James N., xi, 17, 22, 26, 27, 28, 39
Frozen, 6

G H
Godfather, The, 81
Gone with the Wind, 23
Harry Potter and the Philosopher's (Sorcerer's) Stone, 49
heroism, 8
How to Write a Damn Good Novel, 17, 27, 62
How to Write a Damn Good Novel, II, xi, 22, 26, 28, 39
human worth, high, 90

INDEX

humor, 43

I J K L
I, Spy, 55, 71
Indiana Jones, 12
inner conflict, 26
  and Save the cat!, 38
  character choices, 27
  klutziness, 4
  Kryptonite, 52

M
Maass, Donald, 33, 38, 90
motivation
  and backstory, 88
  antiheroes', 81
  for bad actions, 87
  selfish, 70
  selfless, 70
mushy moment, 73
Mystery Man on Film, 12

N O P
noble goal, 28
  creating sacrifices, 36
  establishing, 30
perfect characters, 1
  avoiding, 19
Phineas and Ferb, 10
physical beauty, 5
pity, 26

R
Raiders of the Lost Ark, 12
Rasley, Alicia, 3, 8, 11, 23, 41

reader identification, xi
romance, 69
Romeo and Juliet, 42, 57
Rowling, J.K., 49

S
sacrifice, 28
sad sack characters, 2
  avoiding, 25
  Harry Potter (avoiding), 49
Save the cat
  definition, 35
Save the cat!
  and inner conflict, 38
Save the Cat!, 34
Scarlett O'Hara, 23, 56
Shakespeare, 42
Sherlock Holmes, 64, 90
Snyder, Blake, 34, 44
Spy Another Day series, 55
Spy for a Spy, 55
stakes
  personal, 32
  public, 33
Stevens, Theresa, 80, 81, 89
strengths, 17
Study in Scarlet, A, 64
superheroes, 51
Superman, 52
suspense
  and sympathy, 6

T U V W X Y Z
telling vs showing, 8
Tomorrow We Spy, 56
Too Stupid Too Live, 86

unlovable characters, 79
villain, 72
Weiland, K.M., 73

Thank you for reading!

If you enjoyed this book,
please tell your writing friends & review it online.

To sign up for information on upcoming releases, please visit http://JordanMcCollum.com/newsletter/

Find more character sympathy examples and more at my website:
http://JordanMcCollum.com/books/character-sympathy/

Writing craft classes!

I'm now offering classes on writing craft through my website! Topics include character depth, character arcs, structural self-editing and more!

Class sizes are kept small to feature personal interaction and hand-on help. Lesson materials go beyond an overview of the topics presented to dig into how to apply those techniques in your current work.

Be sure to join my mailing list to be the first to hear about future class schedules and topics!

http://JordanMcCollum.com/newsletter/

The Writing Craft Series

Character Arcs
Out now

In most fiction, the story changes the major characters forever. They learn and grow, ultimately succeeding at the climax of the story because of all they've gained. For a character to truly resonate with readers, he should change and grow over the course of the story.

Tension, Suspense & Surprise
Coming soon

What keeps a reader glued to your novel no matter what the hour? Tension and suspense. Blend these techniques with surprise to keep your readers turning those pages in any genre.

Character Depth
Coming soon

Is your character—and your plot—coming off one-dimensional? Your characters don't have to be philosophers to be "deep." Make your characters come to life and give your readers the immersive emotional experience they crave.

Acknowledgments

Once again, my family has been my rock and constant support as I worked on this book. My husband Ryan and our children, Hayden, Rebecca, Rachel and Hazel, have given me so much time and help for my writing and publishing endeavors. I couldn't do this without you and your support. Writing and teaching writing might make me happy, but you bring me joy.

As always, I have to thank my parents, Ben and Diana Franklin, for instilling a love of learning and literature throughout my life. My sisters, Jaime, Brooke and Jasmine have always been there for me and continue to support and encourage me in all my endeavors. My wonderful critique partners, Julie Coulter Bellon and Emily Gray Clawson, always provide feedback, encouragement and cheerleading whenever I need.

I'm grateful to everyone who has read my blog series on creating character sympathy over the last four years. It was one of my first series on writing craft, and it was my first taste at writing instruction. I was definitely bitten by the writing-about-writing bug! All the people who've comments, posted and shared my writing blog over the years have made it worth all the time and effort. You're too numerous to name individually, but thank you so much.

My friend Marnee Bailey provided help and support all those years ago when I first began learning the principles of character sympathy, and she read those early drafts to offer constructive criticism, and shared her writing knowledge with me over the years. My beta readers, Tonette dela Luna, Arline Holbrook and Morgyn Star, took time and care to read this book and provide me with much needed feedback. Becca Puglisi's feedback and encouragement for *Character Arcs* also proved immensely helpful in writing and editing this book as well.

Most of all, I'm grateful to the wonderful authors and bloggers who have helped me learn more about the craft of writing, giving me the tools to process the nuances of storytelling so I could eventually share some of that knowledge. With this book, special credit must go to James N. Frey's books which helped me so much all those years ago, and to Alicia Rasley and Theresa Stevens, who have shared so much of their expertise through their blog. Their tutelage took my understanding and craft of fiction to another level.

About the Author

PHOTO BY JAREN WILKEY

An award-winning fiction author, Jordan McCollum enjoys teaching through writing conferences, on her writing craft blog at JordanMcCollum.com, and in her Writing Craft series. She has previously served as the Education Director of Authors Incognito (an online writers' support group with over four hundred members). On the fiction side, she is the author of the romantic suspense novels *I, Spy* and *Spy for a Spy*, both of which were named among the five finalists for the 2013 Whitney Awards. She makes her home in Utah with her husband and their four children.

Made in United States
North Haven, CT
19 April 2025